Stations of the Cross

Community Prayer Edition

Timothy Radcliffe

Art by Martin Erspamer

D1520056

LITURGICAL PRESS
Collegeville, Minnesota

www.litpress.org

Nihil Obstat: Reverend Robert Harren, J.C.L., *Censor deputatis*.
Imprimatur: ✠ Most Reverend Donald J. Kettler, J.C.L., Bishop of Saint Cloud, Minnesota. March 24, 2015.

Cover design by Ann Blattner. Illustrations by Martin Erspamer, OSB.

ISBN 978-0-8146-4706-6   978-0-8146-4731-8 (e-book)

Introduction

The Stations of the Cross are a beautiful expression of the core of our faith, which is that Jesus embraced the dramas of every human life, our triumphs and failures, our joys and sorrows. In the Stations, we remember how the Lord is with us, especially when we seem to be stuck and have lost the way forward. He walks with us, trips with us when we stumble, and helps us to our feet again.

Each station recalls a moment when Jesus stopped. A "station" means simply a place of stopping, as trains stop in railway stations. He stops to talk to people in compassion; he stops when he falls to the ground out of exhaustion, unable to carry on; he stops at Golgotha because that is the end of the road. Jesus is close to us when we too are stopped in our tracks and wonder whether we can carry on anymore. We may be halted by illness or failure, by grief or despair. But Jesus carries on, making his slow way to the cross and to the resurrection, and brings us with himself in hope. Let us set out.

Prayer: Gracious God, as we set out with Jesus, as he begins his passion, open our ears to hear his invitation to take up our own crosses every day and follow him. Give us the courage to face the challenges we encounter on the way, free from the paralysis of fear. Strengthened by your grace, may we help each other to our feet. May we be confident that, walking with the Lord, we shall arrive together at the fullness of life and joy, which is our hope and your gift. We ask you this through Christ, your Son and our brother. Amen.

FIRST STATION

Jesus Is Condemned to Death

LEADER: We adore you, O Christ, and we praise you.
PEOPLE: Because by your holy Cross, you have redeemed the world.

Scripture: "[Pilate] said to the Jews, 'Behold, your king!' They cried out, 'Take him away, take him away! Crucify him!' Pilate said to them, 'Shall I crucify your king?' The chief priests answered, 'We have no king but Caesar.' Then he handed him over to them to be crucified." (John 19:14-16)

Reflection: The one thing of which we are sure is that one day we shall die. We all know our birthdays. We also have death days, the annual day of our coming death, but we do not know which day it is. People who are dying often have an acute sense of the gift of being still alive. If we remember that we too are condemned to die, then we may live every day as precious and unrepeatable, with the gifts and graces the Lord will give us today. Lord, give us gratitude for this day, and every day until we die.

Prayer: Jesus, at this moment you stand judged and condemned. You take upon yourself all the accusations that human beings hurl against each other. You bear the contempt that has crushed people throughout the centuries. Give us the courage to be close to those who are condemned and rejected by the world, whether they be innocent or guilty. Now you set off toward your crucifixion. Give us confidence in your love, which is stronger than death and will have the victory. Amen.

SECOND STATION

Jesus Receives the Cross

LEADER: We adore you, O Christ, and we praise you.

PEOPLE: Because by your holy Cross, you have redeemed the world.

Scripture: "And when they had mocked him, they stripped him of the purple cloak, dressed him in his own clothes, and led him out to crucify him." (Mark 15:20)

Reflection: Jesus says that if we are to be his disciples, then we must take up our cross and follow him. That may sound rather masochistic, as if we must positively want to suffer. Sometimes it has made Christianity seem grim. But it means that we dare to embrace the life that is given to us, with its joys and suffering, its blessings and limitations. It is no good wishing that we were someone else. This is our life, a gift from God, and even its rough and hard moments are steps toward happiness.

Prayer: Jesus, now you take upon yourself the burden of the cross and all that weighs us down. Give us the strength to walk onward, uncrushed by whatever is placed on our shoulders. May we help others to endure in the trials and sufferings of their lives, with joy undefeated. Amen.

THIRD STATION

Jesus Falls for the First Time

LEADER: We adore you, O Christ, and we praise you.

PEOPLE: Because by your holy Cross, you have redeemed the world.

Scripture: "He was pierced for our sins,
        crushed for our iniquity.
    He bore the punishment that makes us whole,
        by his wounds we were healed." (Isa 53:5)

Reflection: We all have many "first falls." We may feel ashamed, and in self-defense we may deny the sin altogether, declaring "I am not that sort of person!" But let us remember that Jesus is close to us and has borne the shame of all first fallers and continues to do so. We can then dare to look at ourselves with honesty, knowing that we are indeed just that sort of person. We are not the perfect parents, or the amazing spouses, or the spotless pious priests that we may have imagined. But God smiles on us as we are, warts and all. We may not be perfect but neither are we despicable worms. We are fallible human beings who fumble our way to the kingdom, keeling over from time to time.

Prayer: Jesus, when we fall and feel discouraged, may we know that you are especially close to us then, bearing our shame and giving us the strength to stand up on our feet and begin to walk again. Make our hearts tender toward all those whose falls bring upon them the righteous indignation of others. May the desire for holiness continue to burn within us. Amen.

FOURTH STATION

Jesus Is Met by His Blessed Mother

LEADER: We adore you, O Christ, and we praise you.

PEOPLE: Because by your holy Cross, you have redeemed the world.

Scripture: "As a mother comforts her child,
so I will comfort you;
in Jerusalem you shall find your comfort." (Isa 66:13)

Reflection: The death of a child before his or her parents is outrageous. It contradicts the natural order of things. It is the child who ought to care for his or her parents and bury them. This is the appalling suffering of parents who lose their children in war or to illness. Think of the mothers whose children disappeared during the years of dictatorship in Argentina, Las Madres de Plaza de Mayo, who did not even have the bodies of their children to bury. All this scandalous suffering is embraced by God when Jesus and his mother meet on the way to the cross. Jesus *is* every child lost prematurely, and Mary *is* every parent grieving for his or her child.

Prayer: Jesus, be close to all who lose or become distant from the people they love, especially parents mourning their children. If we are separated from them by death, may we trust in the ultimate victory of God's love, which will gather us together once more. If it is through alienation or misunderstanding, then may we be confident that one day God's grace will cast down every barrier, and we shall be at home with each other in you. Amen.

FIFTH STATION

Simon of Cyrene Helps Jesus to Carry His Cross

LEADER: We adore you, O Christ, and we praise you.
PEOPLE: Because by your holy Cross, you have redeemed
          the world.

Scripture: "As they led him away they took hold of a certain Simon, a Cyrenian, who was coming in from the country; and after laying the cross on him, they made him carry it behind Jesus." (Luke 23:26)

Reflection: Western culture has promoted the ideal of the self-sufficient person who does not need anyone else. We should stand on our own feet. It is humiliating to need others, especially strangers. But this dependency is part of being human, and it is embraced by God in Jesus at this moment. God says to St. Catherine of Siena, "I could well have supplied each of you with all your needs, both spiritual and material. But I wanted to make you dependent on one another so that each of you would be my minister, dispensing the graces and gifts you have received from me." In Jesus, we see God needing us, needing a drink from the Samaritan woman at the well, needing help with carrying his cross. It's okay to be needy.

Prayer: Jesus, may I be unashamed to accept help when I need it, and may I be eager to offer it when others have needs. May our mutual dependence be a source of joy and an occasion of grace, knitting us together in the community of your love. Amen.

SIXTH STATION

Veronica Wipes the Face of Jesus

LEADER: We adore you, O Christ, and we praise you.
PEOPLE: Because by your holy Cross, you have redeemed the world.

Scripture: " 'She has done a good thing for me. . . . Wherever the gospel is proclaimed to the whole world, what she has done will be told in memory of her.' " (Mark 14:6, 9)

Reflection: The face of God became flesh in the face of Jesus, who smiled upon sinners with tenderness. He looked with pleasure on pompous little Zacchaeus up in the tree and decided to stay with him rather than the self-righteous and respectable people. He smiled on Levi, another tax collector, and called him to discipleship. He looked with kindness on Peter after he had betrayed him. But what about us? We do not see his face, and we do not even know what Jesus looked like. We are the Body of Christ, and so we must be his face. It belongs to the ministry of every baptized person to be the face of Christ in the ordinary interactions of our daily lives. It is the small but necessary beginning of all Christian witness. According to the legend, Jesus on the way to the cross found among a crowd of hostile faces one that gazed on him with pity, and to her he gave an image of his face. May our faces be shaped by grace into tenderness and welcome, "true images" of his.

Prayer: Jesus, may I see with your compassion and smile with your radiance, so that your unfailing tenderness is made flesh and blood in me. May I always be alert to those who feel invisible and despised, recognizing that they are your brothers and sisters, sharing your dignity, however much this is concealed by the bruises of this life. Amen.

SEVENTH STATION

Jesus Falls for the Second Time

We adore you, O Christ, and we praise you.

Because by your holy Cross, you have redeemed the world.

Scripture: "Therefore, he had to become like his brothers in every way, that he might be a merciful and faithful high priest before God to expiate the sins of the people. Because he himself was tested through what he suffered, he is able to help those who are being tested." (Heb 2:17-18)

Reflection: Our macho society is tempted to look patronizingly on people who are physically weak. Our Lord shared that physical weakness and blesses it. He also embraces us in our moral weakness. When I am weak, I may discover that I am not alone battling against the wind and the storms. Jesus shared our weakness so that we may share his strength. At the core of each of us is the strong Son of God. In my deepest interiority, God abides, and his grace will lift me up again and again, and put courage back in my heart. Pope Francis said that morality is not "never falling down" but always getting up again. We keep on walking.

Prayer: Jesus, lift me to my feet when I feel that I go can no further. When I feel battered by the storms of life, with neither the energy or strength to carry on, then may I know that you, the strong Son of God, will bear me onward until I arrive at home in God. Amen.

EIGHTH STATION

The Women of Jerusalem

Scripture: "A large crowd of people followed Jesus, including many women who mourned and lamented him. Jesus turned to them and said, 'Daughters of Jerusalem, do not weep for me; weep instead for yourselves and for your children, for indeed the days are coming when people will say, "Blessed are the barren, the wombs that never bore and the breasts that never nursed." ' " (Luke 23:27-29)

Reflection: During his journey to the cross, the only people whom Jesus addresses are women. Even in his agony Jesus feels deeply the pain that will be theirs when Jerusalem is destroyed. He is touched by people's pain, and he enjoys their joy more than they do themselves. God's promise is that he will take out our hearts of stone and give us hearts of flesh (Ezek 11:19; 36:26). A heart of flesh is one that shares another's joy without jealousy and another's sorrow without *schadenfreude*. Unqualified joy is only possible when we no longer see the other person as our rival. Until then our happiness will always be insecure, keeping an eye open for competitors who will knock us off our perch. May the Lord chip off our stony hearts the thick rind of egoism that makes us dead to what others live!

Prayer: Jesus, give me a heart of flesh so I may rejoice with those who rejoice and sorrow with those who are saddened. Peel off the shell of selfishness that holds others at bay, so I may be one with them in their lives, free to act with your own spontaneous generosity. Amen.

NINTH STATION

Jesus Falls for the Third Time

LEADER: We adore you, O Christ, and we praise you.
PEOPLE: Because by your holy Cross, you have redeemed the world.

Scripture: "Three times I begged the Lord about this [weakness], that it might leave me, but he said to me, 'My grace is sufficient for you, for my power is made perfect in weakness.'" (2 Cor 12:8-9)

Reflection: Jesus collapses, crushed. People can be crushed by low wages, wondering whether to eat or keep the house warm. Often they are despised by the media. Jesus' fall brings him close to them so that they too may one day share his glory. Oscar Romero adapted a saying of St. Irenaeus of Lyons: *Gloria Dei vivens pauper*, "The glory of God is the living poor person." There are also those who feel crushed by moral failure, like Peter who denied Jesus three times. Jesus struggles up and carries on, one step nearer to the cross. Then he will lift the burden from Peter, and from us all, with infinite delicacy. Without even referring to his failure, he will give Peter three opportunities to unspeak it: "'Do you love me more than these [others]?'" (John 21:15). Peter will be able to reach below the superficial desire to save his skin to the deep, abiding hunger of his life, the love of his Lord: "'You know that I love you.'" And then he too will be able to stand up and walk again. Whatever we have done, Jesus lifts us to our feet.

Prayer: Jesus, after so many falls, let me not lose hope for happiness and holiness. If you are with me, then I am not doomed to be stuck in the endless repetition of my failures. May your grace bud in the wilderness of my heart. Grant a fresh beginning even today. Amen.

TENTH STATION

Jesus Is Stripped of His Garments

Scripture: "I can count all my bones
They stare at me and gloat;
they divide my garments among them;
for my clothing they cast lots." (Ps 22:18-19)

Reflection: Jesus is stripped of all his clothes. On the cross he will be naked. Even the clothes of Jesus are mere booty, to be shared between the soldiers to supplement their pay. They are part of his "net value." The Son of the Most High God is treated as a piece of property, redeeming all those who are bought and sold, from footballers to sex workers. Who does not have a price? With the eyes of faith, we can see his nakedness otherwise. David stripped to fight Goliath. Jesus, the Son of David, strips to fight against every humiliation that we endure, every shame that makes us shrink. He climbs the cross to win the victory for our dignity.

Prayer: Jesus, I fear to be seen as I am, with my foolish fears and hidden failures. I would be ashamed and wish to hide, like Adam and Eve. But for us you have been stripped naked and borne the jeers of the world. Comfort those who feel despised. May I know that you, who see me as I am, clothe me with your love. Amen.

ELEVENTH STATION

Jesus Is Nailed to the Cross

LEADER: We adore you, O Christ, and we praise you.

PEOPLE: Because by your holy Cross, you have redeemed the world.

Scripture: "When they came to the place called The Skull, they crucified him and the criminals there, one on his right, the other on his left." (Luke 23:33)

Reflection: He deliberately draws close to us in our helplessness. He is inside all our experiences of being lost and astray, so that we may not be victims but victors with him. He was nailed to the cross, nailed firmly to all our failures, identified with everyone who seems to be a let-down, the child who disappoints a parent, the husband or wife who turned out to have feet of clay, the disgraced priest. He embraces all those who feel that God has abandoned them. His strong grace is in all who feel that their lives are coming apart, and that there is nothing they can do. In him, no life is a dead end. This darkest moment, when the sun and the moon do not shine, is a revelation of glory.

Prayer: Jesus, your life had seemed so full of promise, and yet it ended in the disgrace of the cross. Embrace all those who seem to be utter failures. And as you are close to us these dark moments, so may we share with you in the radiance of your resurrection. Amen.

TWELFTH STATION

Jesus Dies on the Cross

LEADER: We adore you, O Christ, and we praise you.
PEOPLE: Because by your holy Cross, you have redeemed the world.

Scripture: " 'My God, my God, why have you forsaken me?' " (Matt 27:46; Mark 15:34)

Reflection: What can we say of anyone's death, since we do not know what it is to be dead? Dying we know, but not death. What possible words can we have for the death of God? The Word of God is silenced. What words do we have? Yet this dead man on the cross is the Word that speaks most loudly of a love beyond imagination. Pain and destitution often make people feel deeply alone and isolated. No one can understand the suffering that we endure. It is beyond sharing. But in Christ, one is never alone. In him God embraces everyone who feels abandoned and betrayed: people struggling with the loss of those whom they love, those who are angry at senseless terminal illness, those who feel that God has let them down. In Jesus, God embraces the absence of God. God has come near to us in our desolation, and so we can come into his presence.

Prayer: Jesus, be with us at the hour of our death. May those who feel abandoned by God know that he is closer than we can imagine. May those who feel that there is no God at all discover his intimate presence. Amen.

THIRTEENTH STATION

Jesus Is Taken Down from the Cross

LEADER: We adore you, O Christ, and we praise you.

PEOPLE: Because by your holy Cross, you have redeemed the world.

Scripture: "In order that the bodies might not remain on the cross on the sabbath, . . . the Jews asked Pilate that their legs be broken and they be taken down." (John 19:31)

Reflection: The Lamb of God, not one of whose bones have been broken, has become an obstacle to the celebration of the feast. He is in the way of religion. Dictatorships and tyrannies often find Jesus inconvenient. Oscar Romero had to be disposed of because he opposed the religion of the government of El Salvador: national security. We may also sometimes find that Jesus gets in the way with his demands for nonviolence and his identification with sinners and the poor. It is tempting to celebrate our comforting religion without the disturbance of its Lord.

Prayer: Jesus, now you are lowered from the cross into the hands of those who loved you and who stayed by your side to the end. May we have the courage to remain faithful to you when it is costly. Grant us to be faithful to all those whom we love, even when we receive nothing in return. Amen.

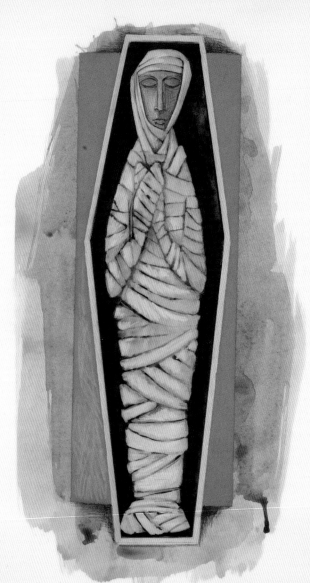

FOURTEENTH STATION

Jesus Is Placed in the Tomb

LEADER: We adore you, O Christ, and we praise you.

PEOPLE: Because by your holy Cross, you have redeemed the world.

Scripture: "Taking the body, Joseph wrapped it [in] clean linen and laid it in his new tomb that he had hewn in the rock. Then he rolled a huge stone across the entrance to the tomb and departed." (Matt 27:59-60)

Reflection: This looks like the end of the story. But Jesus is on the cusp of a new beginning. There lies before him an unimaginable future, which he will share with everyone whose life seems to have reached a final impasse. No dead end can finally defeat God's creative touch. The African-American spiritual asks, "Were you there when they laid him in the tomb?" We were all there, every one of us, when we feared that there was no way forward, when the path was blocked by some great rock. He is there whenever we feel entombed, hemmed in, in the darkness.

Prayer: Jesus, now you are laid to rest in the tomb. May we rest in your love, confident that even when the future is obscure, we nestle in your Father's care. Grant us patient endurance until we hear your final summons to the fullness of life. Amen.

Conclusion

Gracious God, now we have arrived at the end of our journey to the resting place of Jesus. We have been with him as he endured opposition, mockery, failure, suffering, and death. He has thus embraced every upset and defeat that we may face in our pilgrimage through life. Grant us, most generous God, that walking in the way of Jesus, we may attain that joy and freedom to which you call us. We ask you this through Christ our Lord. Amen.